KINDLE

Fire 10

USER GUIDE

FOR **NEWCOMERS**

**User manual for kindle fire 10:
exploring, troubleshooting, and using
Alexa on Fire HD 10 like a pro**

Stephen W. Rock

Dedicated to all my readers

Acknowledgement

Ii want to say a very big thank you to Michael Lime, a 3D builder, my colleague. He gave me moral support throughout the process of writing this book.

Table of Contents

Introduction 10

1 ....**12**

Know your device **12**

Getting started 12

Powering up your Kindle device 17

2 ....**19**

Battery and controls **19**

Charging the device 22

3 ....**24**

Setup and registration **24**

Cloud drive and file storage 24

Setup email.. 26

Contact Setup.. 26

Personalize Kindle Fire HD 10 28

How to set up multiple profiles 29

Using the calendar on Fire HD 10 30

Link Fire HD 10 to Amazon Account 31

Connecting to Bluetooth with your Fire HD 10 32

4 ....**34**

Kindle Fire HD 10 Accessibility features.............**34**

Customize Language and Keyboard...................... 35

Managing Sounds and notifications 37

5..**39**

Reading books on Your Kindle Device **39**

Buying Books from Amazon 39

Borrowing books on Amazon 40

Reading books on your device 41

Getting free books 42

Reading settings 44

Reading features... 45

6 ....**47**

Music and Audio **47**

Adding music files 47

How to listen to music.. 49

Buy and listening to audio books....................... 50

7..**53**

Movies and Videos...**53**

Opening and playing video files 53

Watching videos on YouTube 55

Transferring your video to Fire HD device.......... 58

Renting movies 60

Buying movies 61

8 ....**63**

Managing Device Apps **63**

How to download apps 63

10 apps you should get for your Fire HD 10 66

Buying apps 70

9 ....**71**

Starter guide for Alexa hands-free **71**

Using Alexa.. 72

10 ....**75**

How to uninstall an app **75**

11 ....**77**

Security features **77**

Setting parental controls.................................... 77

Using Passwords and screen lock 81

12 ....**84**

Documents and Camera.....................................**84**

Using the camera 84

Using Documents 86

How to transfer photos and documents to your Fire HD 88

Creating folders in your kindle Fire HD 10 90

13 92

Troubleshooting your kindle fire 92

Problem when starting 92

Keyboard is unpredictable 93

Internal error code 94

EBook vanishes 95

Doesn't connect to computer 97

Blue or purple haze around the edge of scree 99

Fire HD overheats 100

Tablet refuse to charge 101

Device doesn't give sound 102

Fire HD hangs 103

Doesn't connect to Wi-Fi 104

Issues with the battery 105

Email doesn't work 106

Resetting your device 107

14 ....**108**

How to update your device.............................108

Disclaimer 110

About the author...111

Introduction

The title of this book already gives a hint on what the book is about. It is a guide for new users of the Amazon Kindle Fire HD 10 device.

Readers will be introduced into the Fire 10 device proper, learn set up and operation and be taught through basic Kindle fire 10 troubleshooting.

Also, readers will learn how to configure and customize the Fire 10 device to perform several impressive actions, including but not limited to streaming music, reading books, watching movies, managing apps, shopping on Amazon, etc.

Eventually, you'll come to when you'll see how to use Alexa on your fire 10 tablet.

The content of this book are well presented. Steps are outlined to make it easier for readers to identify what to do and how to go about it without any distraction.

This is just another superb user guide from the author's stable. Read and explore.

1

Know your device

Getting started

The Amazon Kindle Fire HD 10 gives users an enhanced experience at an affordable price. But when you first get your Kindle Fire HD, it might strike you as odd. This is just because the operating system it runs on is the Google version. And of course this type is different and not like the sort of android you might know

With this version, Amazon got the opportunity to customize and tweak things to fit their business and brand as an online business. But the fact that it is different doesn't mean that it is hard to use. But if you're finding it a little difficult to set it up, it will be explained here.

Step 1

If you just bought your Kindle Fire HD, or maybe you got it as a gift, you will have to set up the device starting from the very beginning. To start the registration,

1. You want to first select your preferred language and edit your regional settings. After doing that, select **Next**

2. Now will want to connect to a Wi-Fi and go online, you should go through this step. Search for your network and when the name appears, put in the password of the network and **Connect**

3. You will now be asked to enter your email address. This will be the email address that

was used to register your Amazon account. Enter it and hit **Register**

4. Confirm the details of your account. And if by chance you don't have an Amazon account, you can just press **Start Here**. You will be directed to follow the prompts it provides

Step 2

Now you'll want to connect to a Wi-Fi network.

1. Swipe down from the top of the screen and you'll open up the **Quick Settings** area.

2. You should see the icon for Wi-Fi at the upper left corner of the screen, toggle it on.

3. Select the name of your network and input the password

Step 3

The next thing to do is to select your social networks. You have the ability of connecting your Kindle Fire HD with your social accounts like your Facebook or Twitter. This will make it much easier to access your social media

To do this

1. Enter the **Settings**
2. Choose **My Account**
3. Select **Social Account**
4. If it is Facebook that you wish to connect, hit the option to **Connect Your Facebook** and put it the required log in information.
5. You don't have to go through this step. So if you don't want do to, just hit **Next** at the down part of the screen. Move over to the next step

Step 4

You're done

Yeah that's right, your Fire HD is good and ready to be used. But one thing is that when you enter this phase, your device will show up a button for you to **Get Started**. If you choose it, you'll be taken through a quick tutorial of your device.

You have lots of options to discover on your Kindle Fire HD. But the main apps that you will need will be shown in the home screen. And yes there's the web browser – Silk. There are some apps that when you tap them to launch and use, you'll be taken through a tutorial. Just follow the prompts and you'll be good.

If you need to go back to the home screen at a certain time, just hit the home icon and the very bottom of the screen. (it is the circle at the middle)

Powering up your Kindle device

If you just got your Fire HD 10, you want to make sure it is fully charged. Make sure that the battery is not low. If the battery is low, be sure to use the USB cable that came with your Kindle Fire HD 10 to charge it. You want to try at all cost to always use the charger that came with your tablet

After you plug in the cable, leave it for a while to charge. Once the battery is full, you can remove it and power it. To do his

1. Locate the power button. It's the one at the top right of the device.

2. Press and hold it for a few seconds

3. If you want to restart the device, press
   and hold the button for a few seconds and
   a menu will show up on the screen. Tap
   OK to turn off. After device as shut down,
   press the power button to power it up.

2

Battery and controls

While the Amazon Kindle Fire HD 10 comes with a wonderful battery life, you want to do a few things to help you use your device even longer without charging. If you follow these steps your battery will not automatically stop reducing but it will sure boost your battery's life.

Strike down the brightness

We all love high brightness on our screens. Of course that's when you really get the fullpp and splendid display of the fire. You get to view your movies better and the overall presentation is just nice. But if you're really looking to save some battery life, you've got to draw the bright ness down

To decrease the brightness, swipe down from the top of the screen and reduce the slider for brightness

Screen timeout

If your screen timeout is set to a long period of time, you definite won't have much battery to use. This reasons obvious, the device is kept on whether even if you're not using it.

To reduce the time
1. Swipe down from the top of the screen
2. Choose **Settings**
3. Hit **Display**
4. Select **Display Sleep**
5. Change the screen timeout to lower the time

Wireless networks

If you want to save more battery, switch off Wi-Fi or even better, turn on Airplane mode

Location-Based Services

There are some services that run in the background. One of them is the Location-Based services. Even if the fact that the information of your location is being collected doesn't sound creepy to you, it's got to be turned off to save more battery.

1. Go to **More**
2. Then **Location-Based services**
3. Switch it off

Charging the device

After you get your Kindle Fire HD 10, the first thing you want to do is charge it. Dont set any thing up, don't register anything, just charge it. And of course you want to use the cable that came with your Fire HD.

You can use another cable, but it will charge slowly and you'll just spend a lot of time simply charging the battery. It would make no sense using a different cable when the original one is lying around okay.

Your battery will not only charge slowly if you use a different cable, if you charge from your computer, it will also charge slowly.

1. Plug the big end of the cable to the power adapter.

2. Connect the other end of the cable to your Fire HD

3. Now plug the power adapter to an outlet on the wall

If you want to know whether your device is charging, a lightning bolt should show up on the battery at the corner of the screen. If you plug the cable and it the lightning bolt does not appear, then your Fire HD is not charging

3

Setup and registration

Cloud drive and file storage

If you want to upload files and store them for when you need them at a later date, the Amazon Cloud Drive is one way to go. It also allows you to stock documents and you have the opportunity to share them when you want. If you want to get started and use the Amazon cloud drive, it's really simple and you don't have to waste time to start.

If you're one that buys product with your already registered Amazon account, you have the ability to go in and use the cloud drive already. Once you sign in you'll be shown the page for uploading. If you use the Amazon Cloud Dive Storage, you get 5GB storage for free. But of course you can pay to get additional storage space.

To upload files,

1. At the upper left of the screen, you'll see the button for you to **Upload Files**, select it

2. Now, you'll be given four folders to store files. You get **Music, Pictures, Documents** and **Videos**. Select a folder to upload the contents

TO get the files you've uploaded, you can just move to the Amazon Cloud Drive account. You can even play a video with your browser.

Setup email

You can link your Fire HD with your calendar or contacts. But you would have to use your email. If you want to, you may even include more than one email

To setup your email in your Fire HD 10

1. Enter the home of your device
2. Choose Apps and enter email
3. Enter in the password
4. Hit **next**

Contact Setup

When it comes to setting up contacts on your Kindle Fire HD, you may set up a new contact or if you want or you may just import the contacts from your own email

To set up a new contact

1. Fire up the **contact app**
2. Hit **New**
3. Put in the details and info required
4. If you want to move to the next field, press Next
5. Choose Save

To import contacts from email

1. Connect your email to your Fire HD tablet
2. Enter the **Contact app**
3. Choose **Add New**
4. Select an account to import the contacts in your email from

Personalize Kindle Fire HD 10

Add more storage space

Unless you're one that doesn't download anything on your device, your Fire HD becomes loaded up after a while. And if your device doesn't have a lot of storage, you will find that the space will get filled pretty quickly

You could say Amazon anticipated this outcome, they provided a port for a microSD card. What this means is that if your original device storage is filled up, you can just get microSD card with a lot of storage and supplement

Access to movies

Even if you didn't know already, the name Amazon Fire HD should tell you that it's made by Amazon. Bu that doesn't mean it's only from them you can get movies. No, that's why we have

Movies Anywhere. This will enable you to slide into the Apple libraries or even Google libraries

Just install the app, set it up and you'll be able to stream videos, you can also download.

Make it stand

You can make watching movies with your tablet a lot more comfortable by purchasing a case with kick stands or a pen to hold the tablet in standing mode.

How to set up multiple profiles

With your Kindle Fire HD, you can set up multiple profiles and add set up profiles for 2 adults. You even get the chance to setup profiles for four children.

If you want to add a profile

1. Enter the Quick Settings by swipe down from the top of the screen
2. Choose **Settings**
3. Select the **Profiles & Family Library**
4. If you want to include an adult, Choose **Add Adult**
5. If it's a kid you want to add, choose **Add Child** instead

Using the calendar on Fire HD 10

You can create a new event in the calendar of your Kindle Fire HD. But you still get event set in the calendar app by default.

1. Enter the **Calendar**
2. Choose a date
3. Hit **New Event** button to make new event

4. You'll be given the Event form. This will enable you to add the information of the event

5. To add when the event ends, choose **To time**

6. TO add when the event starts, choose **From time**

7. Add in the other information you want to add and when you're done, hit **Save**

Link Fire HD 10 to Amazon Account

As you get your Fire HD and set it up for the first time, you'll be prompted to connect your device to your Amazon account. Not every actually connects at that moment. So if you missed that process you can still link them.

1. Swipe down from the top of the screen and enter the Quick settings
2. Hit **Settings**
3. Select **My Account**
4. Hit **Register**
5. Add the information required for your account
6. Touch **Continue**

You want to make sure you've created an Amazon account before even linking it to your device. But if you have not linked it, you just select **Start Here**

Connecting to Bluetooth with your Fire HD 10

When it comes to Bluetooth matters with your device, you want to make sure that your Bluetooth is near your Fire HD. You also want to verify that your Bluetooth device is compatible with your Kindle fire.

To use Bluetooth

1. Grab your Bluetooth device and fix it to pairing mode
2. Swipe down from the top of the screen on your tablet
3. Choose **Bluetooth**
4. Toggle on **Bluetooth**
5. Touch **More Settings**
6. Select **Pair Bluetooth device**
7. The list of devices that can be found by your Kindle fire will be shown. Choose your Bluetooth devices from the option and comply with the prompts given

4

Kindle Fire HD 10
Accessibility features

You have amazing accessibility features in your Fire HD. Like for example, you can use it to make the text size larger or do something like magnifying the screen. You can also program your device to give you some feedback it you press an app or something

TO make this available,

1. Swipe down from the top of the screen
2. Hit **Settings**
3. Choose **Accessibility**
4. From here you'll be given accessibility features to enable

There's the option for **Screen Readers**, this will enable you to get feedback of items you touch. With **Screen magnifier**, you can zoom in on the screen by performing some actions on the screen. If you would like to make the size of text on your device larger, select **Font size**

Customize Language and Keyboard

To change the language on your tablet,

1. Enter the quick settings by swiping down from the top
2. Choose **Settings**
3. Select **Language & Keyboard**
4. Touch **Language**
5. You can now pick the language you want

You also have the auto-correct feature on your keyboard, to edit this,

1. Enter the **Quick settings**
2. Choose the **Settings**
3. Hit **Language & Keyboard**
4. Then **Keyboard Settings**
5. To enable any option shown, tap it
6. Press **Personal Dictionary** to add certain words in the dictionary of the device.

If you wish to change the language of the keyboard

1. Swipe down to enter the Quick settings
2. Tap **Settings**
3. Choose **Language & Keyboard**
4. Touch **Keyboard Language**
5. Choose a language
6. If you want a new language, hit **Download Language**

Managing Sounds and notifications

With your Kindle Fire HD 10, you can edit and tweak the notification sounds. But there's a limit to the sounds you can change, like you can't change the sound that the device makes when you turn it off or connect it to a charger.

Viewing a notification is as easy as swiping down from the top of the screen. If there's a notification you don't want to see anymore, swipe it. But tap it if you want to view the information about it.

If you would like to change the notification settings,

1. Swipe down from the top and enter the **Settings**
2. Press **Notification & Quiet Time**
3. Select the app you want manage

But that's a long route, quicker way to go about it is to just long-press a notification when it arrives and you'll be taken to the page where you can manage the app's notification.

n

5

Reading books on Your Kindle Device

Buying Books from Amazon

Well since you're downloading, you would want to make sure that you're connected to the internet. If you've got a Wi-Fi network, get connecting

To buy books from Amazon you want to,

1. Enter the home screen on your Kindle Fire HD 10.

2. Along the tabs at the top you should be see one titled **Books**. Tap it.

3. Hit the **Store** that at the upper right of the display

4. Now you can select any book you want. If there's a book that you know the title from memory, you can type it in the search. You can cruise through the store in different categories. If you like non-fiction, go to the category and select your choice

5. When you find one that catches your eye, tap it an you'll be taken to where you can view the details of the book and the price

6. To purchase, hit **Buy**

Borrowing books on Amazon

Good news for those who are Amazon Prime members! You can borrow books from Amazon through the Owners lending library. That's not all, when you borrow from the lending library, the books doesn't get due. You just borrow, load them on your Fire HD and enjoy

1. Go to the Kindle store on your device
2. Look for the title that is available for you to borrow
3. Select **Read For Free**

Okay so you can borrow with no due date, wonderful! But there's a downside. You only get to download one book per month. Unbelievable right? I know. But at least it's an option. When you borrow, don't wait to return. Once you're done, just give it back

Reading books on your device

With the new Fire HD 10, reading is a lot more fun. Ever since Amazon started making reading devices reading got a whole new feel. Not everybody likes carry around books. But with your Kindle Fire HD, you can load it with dozens of books and guess what, it doesn't get heavier.

To open up a book and start reading,

1. Enter the home screen on your device
2. Look for the **Books** tab at the top
3. Enter the book library and choose one to read. To find more books, scroll down.

If the book you chose has been opened by you before, it will start from where you ended last.

Getting free books

Downloading free books is really no hassle. The main work becomes filtering the free ones out. And something is that there are a number of sites to get free Kindle books, But going through the Kindle store is highly suggested, it's from Amazon, the guys who made your Fire HD 10. Plus you can get quite a huge amount of free books from there.

- One easy way to get free books is in the section **Bestsellers in the Kindle store**. Once you're in there you can select **Top 10 Free**. Browse famous tittle till you get to the one that interests you. This list you find here is actually updated a number of times daily.
- Or you can go through another method. This one is really efficient as you can get free books fast. Still in the store, search the words **free Kindle books**.

Reading settings

There are a lot of settings you can edit to make your reading experience better. One of this setting is the blue shade. When you use your tablet at night, the light coming from the screen has been proven to lengthen the time spent before you sleep. Meaning that if you use your tablet, the light will not allow you to fall asleep easily.

That's why it has the **Blue shade**. You know how sunglasses helps your eyes from the sun. That's what Blue shade does to the screen

To use this

1. Slide down from the top to enter the Quick settings
2. Hit **Settings**

3. Choose **Display**

4. Select **Blue shade**

5. Shift the slider to your preference

Other settings you can adjust are the ones that appear on the reading page. To manage these, touch the page one and options will show up at the top. Hit **Settings**. When you choose settings, you will see

- **Font size**: This enable you to change the size of the text you read

- **Color mode**: Change the text and background color

- **Margin**: Edit margin to your taste

- **Font**: Allow you to change the font to one you'll read better with.

Reading features

To Bookmark a page

1. Press the center of the page
2. Hit the button for bookmark
3. The bookmark icon should appear on the page now

To highlight a text

If there's a text that you wish to highlight,

1. Hold down on the text
2. Handles should show up of the edges of the text. If you wish to highlight other text, just drag the handle toward the additional texts.

6

Music and Audio

Adding music files

One easy way to add music on your Fire HD is

through your computer. If you have music files on

your computer, you can just simply transfer them

to your device easily with your trusted cable

To do this, you want to ,

1. Plug the smaller end of the USB cable to
    your tablet

2. Connect the other to your computer

3. When the Fire HD shows up on your
    computer, Open up the **internal storage**

4. Open the music folder in your computer and select the music you want to transfer and copy. To copy on Windows, press Ctrl+C. On Mac, Command+C

5. Open a folder to copy on your Kindle Fire HD folder

6. Press Ctrl+V or Command+V in the folder to paste

If you don't like the idea on USB cables you can still go through the second method and do it online. You'll go through the cloud. With this method, you get a free storage to upload 250 songs. But you can pay if you want more space. You can get a storage space for 250,000 songs.

1. Open a browser and to the Amazon website

2. Sign in to your account

3. Move over to **Your Account**

4. Choose Your **Music library**

5. Click the option at the lower left for Upload your music

6. After your computer has been scanned and music has been found, hit **Upload**

Now to get them on your device

1. Enter the **Music** app
2. Select the **Cloud** tab
3. You'll have the opportunity of getting the songs you just uploaded

How to listen to music

As long as you've loaded your Kindle Fire HD with music, you can listen to them through the Music app. If you want to control and manage the music, you can use the play back controls on the screen.

1. Press **Music** on the home screen of the Fire HD

2. Choose one that you would like to play. You have different tab selections. With **Songs**, you can play all the music

3. If there's a song that you would like to play, tap it. You can then control the songs with the controller that appears on the screen.

If the volume gets too loud, or too low for your liking, you can always adjust it to your preference with the volume buttons.

Buy and listening to audio books

Not only do you get to read books, but you can also get someone to read to you. You just move to the Audiobook library and you'll have the opportunity of buying and listening to audiobooks through audible.com. And if you've already gotten an audiobook, it'll be shown.

1. In the home screen of your Fire HD, hit the tab for **Audiobooks**
2. From here you can see the books you've purchased before, if want to get a new book, Tap **Store.**
3. To look for books, you can move over to **Audible best Sellers.** From here you'll be able to cruise through top books. Or you can just head over to the search and type in the name of an audiobook.
4. Once it presents itself, tap it. You'll now get options of payment and be able to listen to a brief sample
5. Once you purchased, you can then move to the library an download.

Now it's already downloaded on your device, so you don't need to be connected to the internet before you can listen to it.

7

Movies and Videos

Opening and playing video files

If you want to play videos on your Kindle Fire HD, you've got to actually have videos. And that's no hassle. You can head over to the Amazon store and get videos. If you like streaming, you've got Netflix. And there's another good news for Amazon Prime members, they have the option of getting free movies.

If you already have videos, on your device, playing videos is only a matter of tap this tap that.

1. Tap **Videos**
2. Choose **Library**

3. Look for a video or movie that you're interested in watching at the moment and tap it

4. The video should start playing already. If you've already started watching the video previously, you'll be asked to either resume from where you stopped last or begin afresh

For those who want to stream a video that's been already stored in the cloud,

1. Tap **Videos** in the home screen of the Fire HD

2. Hit the **Library** at the top right of the display

3. Hit the **Cloud** tab

4. Now you have the option of to choose something to open

5. With movies, once you tap it, the information about the movie will be revealed and you'll be able to download it.

It the movie is one that you've already downloaded, you be able to watch it.

6. With TV shows, you will select **Buy** and you can download the full season. Or if you want to get just some episode, you'll see the list of the episodes

7. Tap **Watch Now** and you'll be able to manage the controls for playback

8. If you already watched the movie to an extent, choose Resume. To start the video from the beginning, Select **Play from beginning** instead

Watching videos on YouTube

Everyone loves to watch YouTube videos. You can move to the website and keep browsing between different channels and videos. Some for education others just to entertain ourselves and relax.

So you will not be so happy to know that YouTube is not in the boundaries of what your Kindle Fire HD can do. This is because the **Google Play Store** doesn't exist in the Fire HD. But that not the end of the line. No we can do something about it.

You just need to download some apps do some settings and you should get your YouTube.

1. Swipe down from the top of the screen and choose **Settings**
2. Hit **Security**
3. Beneath the segment for **Advances,** toggle on the option for **Apps from Unknown sources**
4. A message should pop up now. This is to warn you that this can do damage to your

device. If you're willing to take the risk, tap **OK**. But if you're scared that something can happen to your device, just simply **Cancel**. This is your choice to make, so you can't start blaming anyone if something happens.

5. If you selected **OK**, move to the browser and search in the bar **YouTube apk**. Choose from the options that show up and download it

6. Now you would need **ES File Explorer**. If you don't have the app, you can just download it.

7. Enter the ES File Explorer app and select **Local**

8. Choose **Downloads**

9. Press the **YouTube apk** you downloaded on your device.

10. Hit **Next** to install the apk

YouTube should show up in the app section now. But since it wasn't meant to work with Kindle devices, it may not work as you would expect. If you're facing problems with it, you can download **Google Play Store.**

Transferring your video to Fire HD device

As you already know, you can use your Kindle Fire HD to stream movies and TV shows. But streaming is online. You must have internet connection before you can have the chance to stream anything. But if you have movies or videos on your computer, you don't have to still download them in your device, just copy them.

If you transfer videos to your device, you can watch it offline without connecting to the internet. You Kindle can support the popular format, 3GP and MP4 movies. It can also play VP8

Copying videos from your computer to your device is just the same as copying music files

1. Plug the USB cable to your computer
2. Take the other end of the cable and connect it to your Fire HD.
3. After your computer recognizes your tablet, open it up in the computer.
4. After opening up your device in the computer, select the folder you want to put the videos in.
5. Choose the videos you want to send from your computer and copy
6. Move the Kindle folder you want to copy into and paste

Renting movies

It's very easy to rent videos on Amazon using Prime videos. You can rent movies or TV show that are available for rent. But as the name implies, you only get to watch to a specified period

1. In the home screen, tap Videos
2. Search for the videos you wish to rent. You can type the name in the search field or enter the store
3. When the details of the video is being shown, hit the option for **Rent**

You stream to watch the videos you rent or if you would prefer, you can just download so you can view it offline.

There's this term they call **X-ray**. It helps to find information about the actors and actresses in the movie. But you should note that not all movies are equipped with X-ray. If know if a movie supports it, you will see in the details saying "Includes X-ray"

Buying movies

Not everyone likes the idea of renting. If you want to purchase them instead, you can buy them and watch anytime you want. You don't have to worry about returning anything

To a get a Prime video

1. Enter the Prime video app

2. Go through the categories to find one you like. Or you can search the title in the search bar

3. After you've tapped the video and opened the details, Hit **More Purchase Options**

4. Select **Buy**

When you would like to watch all what you've downloaded, head over to the **Video library** and you'll find them there.

8

Managing Device Apps

How to download apps

Something great about the Kindle Fire HD 10 is that while you can read books, you can do a whole lot more. You not just confined to reading books, at least we just talked about watching movies and listening to music. And that not just all this fire can do, it can also download apps and play games.

When it comes to getting apps, you have to two main methods. Any one you use still gets you your beloved application.

One way is to

1. Enter the Amazon website and go to the Amazon Appstore

2. Select the app you want

3. Inside the page for the app, move to the **Deliver** dropdown and choose your own device

4. Select the option to **Get App**

This way, the app is transferred to your Fire HD

Another way is to

1. Enter the home screen of your device

2. Go to the **Appstore**

3. Scan through the options till you find an app you wish to get. You can also hit the search bar to type in the name of the app

4. After finding the app, tap the option to **Get App.**

5. To download it, hit **Download**

There's another way to apps on your kindle. But this is not from amazon. You you'll be going through other websites. You will soon notice that not all the apps are in Amazon's Appstore. If threes a certain app you want to get and you can find it in the Appstore, just visit other websites.

1. First we've got to make sure your device will allow the app to be installed. So move to the **Settings**

2. Select **Security**

3. Tap the option to allow **Apps from Unknown Sources** and toggle it on. If it brings up a message and you're afraid of what this action might do to your device, just stop at this point.

4. For the brave ones who didn't stop, visit **APKMirror** on a browser

5. Look for what you want to download select the option to download

6. If you have a file manager, go through it and find the just downloaded apk and install

10 apps you should get for your Fire HD 10

Alarm For Me

Gone are the days of getting a physical alarm clock. Who needs it anyway? You've got your Fire HD 10. When you get **Alarm For Me** on your Fire HD, you can select the tone of the alarm, switch the snooze to your liking and you could even get weather reports.

Bitdefender Antivirus Free

These days, the chances of viruses getting into Android devices are pretty high. And as you know, your Fire HD is runs on Android OS. But wouldn't it feel safe if you've got a guard waiting at the entrance and blocking the unfit from entering your tablet. That's why you should get the Bitdefender antivirus app. And it's even for free.

ES File Explorer

You really should have this file manager on your device. It just does the work of arranging your files for you. Your life will be so much easier with ES File Explorer. With it you can view and take notice of all the files on your tablet.

iHeartRadio

For those who wish to stream radio on their tablet,, iHeartRadio is the way to go. It lets you listen to your favorite radio stations and channels. You get to hear hosts who talking about virtually anything. Be it Comedy, Sorts, Shows or just Podcasts

Pinterest

In your Kindle Fire HD, you can get the free Pinterest. This is a social site where you can create boars and store images. You can also get to search for ideas.

Spotify

The popular music app allows you just get almost any song. If you want it for free, you can get it. But you also get ads, Switch to Premium to do away with the ads

Township

Okay this one's more of a game but it's really cool. You get to manage a whole town. And by manage I mean grow animals, build factories, plant crops, make money and all the other stuffs you do in a town.

AccuWeather

For a free app, Acuweather does offer a lot of features. You can get forecast by the minute, alerts about the weather or even a two-week forecast. Everything is just so organized.

Evernote

Everyone has got to take notes at some point. What's even better is that with Evernote on your Fire HD, you can connect your notes to your accounts that you can view them anytime, any where

Crackle

With Crackle, you get access to a long list of movies that you can watch from your Fire HD. You also get to watch TV shows

Buying apps

When you decide to get apps and you visit the Appstore, you may see some apps that you've got to pay to get them. If it's an app you really want and you are willing to buy,

1. Enter the information page for the app.
2. Select the Price. To know if the app is the type you can get for free, you'll see **Free** and not the price
3. Choose **Buy App**
4. Finish the purchase and start the download of the app
5. If you would like to see the app immediately, choose **Open**
6. If you didn't choose **Open**, you can get to the app later in the app library

9

Starter guide for Alexa hands-free

On September 2017, Amazon released Alexa hands-free. If that sounds too much, what this means is that you can access Alexa with actually touching your device.

Why many love this hands-free Alexa is because it's so easy. If hands-free is not enabled, you would need to use the home button to access Alexa and make say your command. If your hands are busy you want to play an Audiobook, have to wash and dry them first before you can tap and tell her to play.

But when you have hands-free enabled, you just have to say the word

So to enable,

1. Swipe down from the top to get to the Quick settings
2. Choose **Settings**
3. Select **Alexa** in the **Device** section
4. Switch **Hands-Free Mode** on

Using Alexa

With Alexa on your Fire HD, you get to play music, ask different questions, search for stuff and even shop with Alexa. If you want to enable Alexa on your device you just have to,

1. Swipe down from the top of the screen

2. Hit the **Settings**

3. Select **Alexa**

4. Toggle on **Alexa**

Now if you want to access Alexa to give a task, press and hold the home icon until a blue line is shown. When the blue line shows, it means you're ready to roll with Alexa. You can make a request, ask a question, or send out a command

If you don't want to press the home screen, you can just enable hands-free mode as we discussed earlier.

For those using a password or a PIN, you would have to enter your PIN or password to use some feature of Alexa. And if you don't want to hands free to be enabled when the screen is in locked mode, you can just

1. Swipe own to enter the Quick settings

2. Tap **Settings**

3. Touch **Alexa**

4. Choose **Hands-Free lock Screen Access**

When you've enabled Hands-Free, you can wake Alexa by simply saying 'Alexa'. But you can change it if you wish. Though there are not many options to alter it to, but you can you choose 'Amazon'

To change the word you say to wake Alexa, you want to first enable Hands-Free mode. After that,

1. Enter the Quick settings by swiping down from the top

2. Hit **Settings**

3. Choose **Alexa**

4. Tap **Wake word**

5. Select the wake word you want

10

How to uninstall an app

If you want to uninstall an app you have 2 ways

to go about it,

1. Form the home screen of the tablet,
    choose **Apps**

2. Now, touch the Device Button

3. All the apps on your tablet will appear at
    this point. If there's an app you want to
    uninstall, long press the app

4. Hit **Remove from device**

5. To confirm, Select **OK**

If the app does not uninstall correctly, you can
just use this next method to get rid of the
application

1. Move to **Settings**

2. Choose **Applications**
3. To find the app you want to remove, Hit **All Applications**
4. Scroll and choose the app
5. Press **Uninstall**
6. Confirm your installation

\

11

Security features

Setting parental controls

A fire tablet for your child can make a wonderful present and you may have gotten one already. They will surely enjoy their time with it. It's a good way to hone their reading skills. And not only reading, they can also play games, listen to songs or watch videos. They can even use some fun apps.

But with such enjoyment they have, you want to place some restrictions. You have to limit them from viewing stuff that they are not supposed to.

And that's what you'll do with the parental controls

If you want to set parental controls, you need to log in with your Amazon account one that particular tablet and you should have created your own profile. You can do this is you haven't, go to **Settings** and choose **My Account**

Now to set it up,
1. Go to the **Settings**
2. Move to **Parental controls** and turn it on
3. Enter in your passwords. Whatever password you put make sure it's not something they can guess
4. You'll be able to stop them from entering the browser, using email and other settings you don't want them to touch
5. If you choose **Set Restricted Access**, you'll be able to determine what time the device will be unavailable

You can also set multiple profiles. What makes this helpful is that if you don't want your kid to see what stuff you're doing on the tablet, you can just set a password. With this, they will not be able to get to your own profile.

1. Move to **Settings**
2. Select **Security**
3. Toggle on **Lock Screen Passcode**
4. Now you can set your password

If you want to create your child's profile,

1. Still go to the **Settings**
2. Select **Profiles & Family Library**
3. Tap the option to **Add a Child Profile**
4. Now you'll be asked to add the info about the child like their name and gender
5. **FreeTime** can be used for children for children under 9, or you can choose **Fire**

For Kids, any one that is available in your region

6. Select **Teen Profiles** if the kid is older than 9

7. You can now choose the items that the child will be able to access. You can choose the type of books, apps or videos.

After creating the profile, if you want to access it, swipe down from the top of the display. At the top right choose the icon for profile. If you choose your child's profile, you would notice that the interface will be not be the same. They will be able to see part that shows the items you allowed for them to use

But if they choose your own adult profile, they'll be prompted to put the password before they can continue.

Why this method is nice and serves a control is that the contents that you kid can access are the ones you set as available. Anyone that you didn't not choose, will not be accessible. If you chose FreeTime, any procedure that will have to do with purchases, will be restricted. In short, it will help keep you child safe

Using Passwords and screen lock

One main reason why people use password and PINs on their devices is because they don't want anyone to take a look at their contents without their consent. Strangers can gather information about you when they get hold of your device.

SO to prevent that, you need to use a means to block the unfit from gaining access to your Fire HD. When you set passwords or PINs, they stop the person on their tracks and they can't do anything useful with your device. The passwords appear on the lock screen and that only shows the time with notifications

Anyone who wants to access your profile must enter the password. But they can change the profile selecting the profile symbol. from the lock screen you can still view notifications when you try to swipe down. But if you don't want that, you set a password to protect notifications

To set a PIN or password

1. Swipe down and select **Settings**
2. Choose **Security &Privacy**
3. Move and toggle on **Lock Screen Password**
4. Now you'll be asked to generate a password or PIN. Whatever you're putting just make sure it's not something an infant

can guess like 1111. To make your passwords more secure, use a mixture of bother letters and numbers. Or you can even spice it up and add some special characters. Who would guess that some punctuation marks will be in your passwords

12

Documents and Camera

Using the camera

All this while we've talked about so many lovely things you can do with your Fire HD 10 but we haven't talked about one cool feature – Taking pictures and videos. Your Fire HD comes with a set of cool cameras.

It's in the front camera by default. This can be very useful when making some video calls. You can use your camera to take awesome photos and shoot videos right from the Camera app.

1. In the home screen, choose **Photos**

2. To fire up the camera, touch the Camera icon

3. You should be in the camera now. Make sure that the camera icon is selected

4. Now to take a picture, direct the camera to face the object and press the shutter button. It's circular

5. To show that a picture has been taken, a thumbnail should show up on the screen. You can select it to view the image

6. There's a menu you can tap for you to get the option to either delete or to share the photo.

You should note that once you take a photo, it will automatically be sent to you Amazon Drive Account. So once you're connected to a network, the photos will br transferred to your account. To cancel this,

1. Enter **Photos** and choose **Menu**

2. Select **Settings**

Using Documents

Among the tabs on you see on the home screen of your device is the docs library. Once you send a document to your Fire HD, it will be stored in this library. You get the opportunity to move the documents to the favorite section. You can also send them to the Cloud though your computer

If you want to get a document on your Fire HD, just transfer from your computer. But the thing with documents is like just like photos and videos you get different types of format. But your tablet boasts of being able to support a lot of format. If you have a docx, PDF, HTML or rtf format, you're good to go.

To get documents on your Kindle Fire HD, you can send them to your Kindle address and then download it with your tablet. While you Kindle fire can view these different formats, it can't edit. You need to get a different app to edit your documents.

If you want to get your Kindle address you have to go through the Amazon website.

1. Grab a PC, enter the Amazon website and sign in to your account
2. Move to **Manage Your Content And Devices**
3. Go to **Personal Document Setting** in **Settings**
4. You should see your Kindle email address in the section for **Send-to-Kindle Email Settings**
5. You can change it by selecting settings **Edit**

How to transfer photos and documents to your Fire HD

Transferring of documents form your computer to your Fire HD is really easy. All you need is the USB cable that came with your kindle fire. You'll be able to transfer both photos and documents.

If you want to send content of kindle to your computer, you can just use the option for Manage your Content and Devices.

1. Move over to **Manage your Content and Devices** In your amazon account.

2. Look for the content. And choose **Download & transfer via USB**. It's In the dropdown for **Actions**

3. After selecting that, choose your kindle and **Download**

4. The content will be downloaded to your computer

To transfer to your Fire HD through USB,

1. Get your computer and move to the folder where the content you want to transfer is
2. Plug the USB cable to your computer and to your Fire HD. TO find your tablet in the computer, go to the place you find a normal external drive.
- For example in Windows, you'll find it in **My computer** or **This PC**
- For Mac, it will be in the desktop. That's after you've installed an application that will help you transfer content to your tablet. You can get **Android File Transfer**
3. Open up kindle in the computer and click s**Internal storage**

4. Open the folder for the content in your computer and drag it into the folder in the internal storage

5. You're done! The content should now be in the folder you selected in your kindle fire

Creating folders in your kindle Fire HD 10

Everyone starts installing, downloading and transferring files to their kindle fire when they get them. What fun will the device be if you don't load it up? Even if you want to listen to music or watch movies, you'll still have to put books or documents.

And with all this loading, comes mess. To deal with his mess one app many love to use is the **ES File Explorer**. This lovely app is a lifesaver. You can create folders to store all the different section of your content in. Slide in to the **Appstore** and get it

1. After installing the ES files Explorer move over to the Tab for Apps
2. Tap the icon to open it
3. Once ES File Explorer is open, enter the menu and you'll be able to create files and sort them to the order you want

13

Troubleshooting your kindle fire

Problem when starting

There's this problem that users complain about.

They say that when they try to start their kindle Fire HD, it might hang or freeze. Sometimes they might not be able to put it on

1. One thing to do is to locate the power button and long press it. Hold it down for about 20 seconds and after a while, press the power button to put it on. There's a chance that the problem will disappear after this.

2. Press and hold the power key till the tablets turns off. When you're sure that the device is switched off, connect it to the charger and then turn it on with the power key. Don't turn it on if your battery is low, leave it to charge for a few hours

Keyboard is unpredictable

The issue where the keyboard of the kindle fire types random letters or just complete jargons is no news. Sometimes it just deletes words you've typed or move to the next page by itself

1. This can just be solved with microfiber cloth. As you use your tablet, oils form your finger and dust can gather on the surface of the screen and confuse the

keyboard. Use the cloth to clean the surface of the screen

2. For those using screen protectors, make sure that there are no bubbles under the protector. Use a card to smoothen them out

3. Restart your device my long pressing the power key for 40 seconds

4. Last resort is the option to factory reset. In **settings,** Go to **Device** and tap **Reset Factory Defaults**

Internal error code

As some use their device, they may get the code saying that **An internal error has occurred** as they try to open up some apps. They might get another massage saying that they have poor network connection.

1. First you want to put your router off. After a while put it on again
2. Restart your fire by holding the power key till it shuts down and putting it on again
3. Select **More**
   - Hit **Applications**
   - Then **Installed Applications**
   - Select the app showing the problem
   - Choose **Force stop** and **Clear Data**
4. Ensure that your date and time are set accurately. To set it
   - Swipe down and hit **More**
   - Select **Date and time**

EBook vanishes

It's been reported that when users try to reboot their device, they lose their ebooks. Some say that they don't open when they're offline. Some of the things you could to is,

1. Check if you've installed **Google Play Store** on your device. IF you have, then there's a chance that that's the main issue. No you don't have to uninstall it.

   - Open up the **Play Store** and enter the kindle app page
   - Uninstall the kindle app.
   - In the main page select the menu (it 3 lines at the upper left)
   - Hit **Settings**
   - Select **Auto-update apps**
   - Choose **Do Not auto-update apps**

   If you want to update your apps, you just do it manually go to the 3 lines again and tap **My apps & games**. Go to **Updates** and update the apps you want to be updated. Make sure you leave out the Amazon apps

2. Another thing is to go to the

- **Settings,**
- Then **Apps & Games.**
- Tap **Manage All Application**
- Look for and tap the kindle app
- **Clear cache** and then **Force stop** the app
3. For those without Google play store, You can just sync your books. After that turn off your device with the power button and turn if on again to see if everything is fine.

Doesn't connect to computer

While transferring documents form the computer to the kindle is a piece of cake for some, for others things just don't go right. As they try to transfer between both devices, they might get a response that a device has disconnected.

In fact it doesn't even get the chance of connecting in the first place

1. Of course the first things you do is restart your device. In fact do the same for both devices. Turn off your computer and your kindle fire. After a few seconds, put them back on. Try to connect together to see if that works

2. Okay if that didn't work, then we can say it's the cable. Make sure that you're using the cable that came with your tablet. The chance of a different cable working with your kindle is low. And if you're using the original cable, check if you find any wires that are exposed.

3. Don't use cables if they don't work. You can always send them through email. No hassle.

Blue or purple haze around the edge of scree

This is no new problem. Many have complained about it. The thing is that as they use their device, they may find a bluish or purplish color surrounding the edge of the display. You might not notice this effect at first, but when you move to a page with a white back ground it becomes fully visible.

Amazon has announced that the reason why this appears is because there happens to be a problem with the parts. For those experiencing this, make sure to contact Amazon. They can replace it the faulty device for you.

Fire HD overheats

As some use their kindle fire, it may start to overheat. It may become warm as you try to touch it. When it becomes warm like this, it does not mean that your tablet Is faulty

1. If the problem is that the tablet becomes warm as it's charging, then you might not be using the charger that came with the device
2. It might be that the processor is busy. At this point, you want to start to quit the opened apps one by one
3. Having a cooling application to cool your battery when it boils like this is a good option. You may decide to use Coolify. But if it still becomes warm, make sure to

replace it, as when batteries get to that point, they may explode

Tablet refuse to charge

This problem can be heartbreaking. This because everyone has to charge their device at some point . When it doesn't charge the device becomes kind of useless. You can manage the battery left, but it will still go off one day.

1. To solve this, be sure that the cable you're using is the one that came directly with your Fire HD. While a different cable can lead to slower charging, it can also lead to no charging. Find your original cable and charge with it

2. Kindle fires are known for their ports that tend to become loose. It may not hold the

charger well. You want to try to push the charger well into the port.

3. Restart you device. Use the power key to turn it off and after a while turn it on

4. If after all doing, it still doesn't charge, make sure you contact Amazon support.

Device doesn't give sound

1. First of don't dig in any settings. Make sure that your volume is turned on. There's a chance you may have done so my mistake. Use the volume up button to increase.

2. To know if the speakers are faulty, plug headphones and notice it that produce sound. If it does then there's a chance that the fault I from the inbuilt speakers.

3. If you use a case, make sure that it is not blocking the speakers form giving audio

4. Make sure to fix the headphone jack well if sound doesn't come from it. You can adjust it a little, it might be unstable

Fire HD hangs

1. If you start to use your tablet and it functions slowly or hangs, just turn it off and on again. Restarting your devices is a sure way to get rid of hanging

2. Make sure that the latest software is on your device

3. If you have something downloading, that may be the reason for the hanging. If the item you're downloading is heavy, make sure you don't use your deceive. Put it down for it to finish

Doesn't connect to Wi-Fi

1. Don't put the blame on your tablet yet. Check out if the Wi-Fi network has a problem by taking another device to connect to the same network. If it connects, then your kindle is at fault. But if it doesn't them contact your network provider

2. Maybe all you have to do is start the connection again. Turn of the Wi-Fi makes sure it disconnects completely and try to connect again

3. Put your fire tablet off and after a while put it back on

4. When airplane mode is turned on, Wi-Fi will not work. Swipe down from the top of the screen and select **Wireless** then toggle

of **Airplane mode.** After switching Airplane mode off, try connecting back to the network again.

Issues with the battery

Some have complained that as they use their kindle fire, the battery just decreases by itself unexpectedly

1. Try restating your device. Press and hold the power key till it goes off and turn it on
2. You have to let go of some apps that cause this. After figuring out the app that causes this,
- Choose **Apps & Games** in the **Settings**
- Select **Manage All applications**

- Uninstall the app that is eating the battery. If you don't know the app, you can try uninstalling al the apps
3. TO reduce the chance of apps refreshing in the background put your device in Airplane mode

Email doesn't work

Some have tried to set their email accounts on their Fire HD. But it doesn't work. While it doesn't not work at all for some, others say that it works for certain time before stops giving updates.

1. As you know, email and internet work together. Without being connected to the internet, email won't refresh and bring new messages.
2. The main reason why this happens is because of the email app. The default app

may not be working. Try to use a different
mail app to be able to receive emails

3. Now you may have to do a factory reset

Resetting your device

1. Enter the **Settings**
2. Select **Device Options**
3. Then Hit **Reset to factory defaults**
4. Choose **Reset**

14

How to update your device

First you want to know the version you use currently

1. Select **settings** when you swipe down form the top of the display
2. Choose **Device option**
3. Select the option that says **System Update**

Now to get the update

1. In Amazon, move to the page for **Kindle Software Update** and choose your device
2. Choose the option to **Download Software update**
3. After download plug a cable to your tablet and then to your computer

4. Select the update you downloaded and copy it

5. Paste it tin the **internal storage** in your Fire HD

6. Disconnect your device and select **more**

7. Hit **Device** then **About**

8. Choose **update**

Disclaimer

In as much as the author believes beginners will find this book helpful in learning how to use an Kindle device, it is only a small book. It should not be relied upon solely for all Kindle tricks and troubleshooting.

About the author

Stephen Rock has been a certified apps developer and tech researcher for more than 12 years. Some of his 'how to' guides have appeared in a handful of international journals and tech blogs. He loves rabbits.

Facebook page @ Newcomers Guide

Also by the Author

1. IPHONE USER MANUAL FOR NEWCOMERS: All in one iOS 12 guide for beginners and seniors (iPhone, 8, X, XS & XS Max user guide)\
2. APPLE WATCH USER GUIDE FOR NEWCOMERS: The unofficial Apple Watch series 4 user manual for beginners and seniors
3. 3D PRINTING GUIDE FOR NEWCOMERS
4. SAMSUNG GALAXY S9 PLUS USER MANUAL FOR NEWCOMERS
5. WINDOWS 10 USER MANUAL
6. KINDLE FIRE HD MANUAL FOR NEWCOMERS